A CONCISE SUMMARY OF **ERIC**

The Lean Startup

...in 30 minutes

A 30 MINUTE EXPERT SUMMARY

GARAMOND
— PRESS —

TABLE OF CONTENTS

INTRODUCTION

Overview

The majority of startup companies fail.

According to Eric Ries, the author of *The Lean Startup,* a startup can reduce their odds of failure by implementing the Lean Startup method. At its roots, the Lean Startup method aims to decrease the risk of failure and increase the likelihood of success by applying the principles of lean manufacturing to the field of entrepreneurship.

The Lean Startup method provides startups with a framework for generating product hypotheses, rapidly testing these hypotheses on customers, and then determining whether to further refine the product or shift resources toward a new product direction. This process is designed to increase the speed of learning and decrease the waste of valuable resources.

About the Author

Eric Ries is a Silicon Valley entrepreneur and co-founded and served as CTO at IMVU, his third startup of many. *The Lean Startup* is his first book; he is also the author of the popular blog, *Startup Lessons Learned.* He was named one of the Best Young Entrepreneurs of Tech by *Business Week* in 2007 and honored with a Tech Fellow award in the category of Engineering Leadership in 2009. He has advised a number of companies, ranging from small startups to venture capital firms, on business and product strategy. He is also an Entrepreneur-in-Residence at Harvard Business School. The Lean Startup methodology has been reported on in *The New York Times, Wall Street Journal, Harvard Business Review,* and *Huffington Post.*

How the Book Came About

Throughout his early career as a computer programmer, Ries built a number of products that failed to be adopted by consumers. As a programmer, he tended to see solutions (and therefore problems) from a technical angle, not from a managerial or entrepreneurial viewpoint. Upon further investigation, however, Ries understood that the problems were not technical, but rather the failure of the business processes he was employing.

To better understand the causes of his repeated failures, Ries evaluated the processes of various industries in search of methods that could revolutionize the entrepreneurial process. In discovering a lean manufacturing process, the *Toyota Production System,* he was introduced to a new way of thinking and the framework for the Lean Startup method was born. Ries' book *The Lean Startup* is the result of both his own personal Lean Startup successes and the widespread growth of the Lean Startup movement, from early-stage startups to Fortune 500 boardrooms.

START

Overview

There is too much uncertainty in a startup to blindly follow a business plan and hope that customer needs are met along the way. Instead, the Lean Startup method shows entrepreneurs how to establish an agile process that iteratively develops a product based on direct customer feedback.

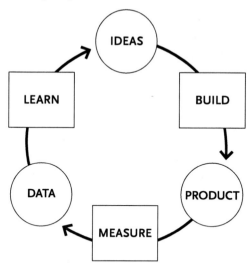

The *Build-Measure-Learn* feedback loop

Building a successful startup begins with the implementation of the *Build-Measure-Learn* feedback loop. Iterations of this loop provide continuous customer feedback, enabling entrepreneurs to constantly make adjustments during product development.

> *"... the Lean Startup is a new way of looking at the development of innovative new products that emphasizes fast iteration and customer insight, a huge vision, and great ambition all at the same time."*
>
> — Eric Ries, *The Lean Startup*

Chapter Summary

The Lean Startup method is inspired by Toyota's revolutionary lean manufacturing system. Lean manufacturing, which advocates a just-in-time production process, employs rapid learning to accelerate production cycles. For startups, this method recommends using rapid customer learning to accelerate product development cycles. The cyclical process of repeated learning and product development that results is what Ries calls the Build-Measure-Learn feedback loop.

The Build-Measure-Learn feedback loop helps startups focus their efforts on *value-creating activities*, which are activities that validate the creation of value for customers. In contrast to following a business plan based on initial (and often unproven) assumptions, each iteration of the Build-Measure-Learn feedback loop aims to gather incremental qualitative or quantitative customer data and use it to inform and improve a product's strategy. To guide the development of a product, startups should dedicate their efforts towards this iterative process, which Ries calls *tuning the engine.*

"The Lean Startup method ... is designed to teach you how to drive a startup. Instead of making complex plans that are based on a lot of assumptions, you can make constant adjustments with a steering wheel called the Build-Measure-Learn feedback loop."

— Eric Ries, *The Lean Startup*

Chapter 1: Key Points

- The Lean Startup method is inspired by Toyota's lean manufacturing system.

- Entrepreneurs should employ the *Build-Measure-Learn* feedback loop, an iterative process that captures customer data and uses it to inform adjustments in product strategy.

- *Value-creating activities*—activities that identify what customers find valuable (and thus are willing to pay for and/or spend time using)—should be prioritized when developing products.

DEFINE

Overview

In order to maintain relevance and sustain growth, all institutions should utilize the Lean Startup method to create an environment that fosters entrepreneurship and entrepreneurial activities. While an "entrepreneur" is typically thought to be a founder of a new startup, Ries explains that entrepreneurs are visionary employees determined to create new products and ventures in companies of all sizes. By empowering these entrepreneurs with a lean development process, even the largest companies can drive innovation.

"Anyone who is creating a new product or business under conditions of extreme uncertainty is an entrepreneur."

— Eric Ries, *The Lean Startup*

Chapter Summary

The Lean Startup method applies lean manufacturing techniques to the process of innovation. These techniques can be applied in businesses across all sectors, from Fortune 500 companies and government organizations to nonprofits, because entrepreneurs are everywhere. Entrepreneurs, as defined by Ries, are the visionaries within all organizations, independent of size, stage, or sector.

Startups are often armed with brilliant ideas, but must utilize process to convert these ideas into successful products. In the same way, traditional management must learn to cultivate entrepreneurs from within larger organizations in order to stay relevant in the modern economy.

"Leadership requires creating conditions
that enable employees to do the kinds of
experimentation that entrepreneurship requires."
— Eric Ries, *The Lean Startup*

A company seeking long-term economic growth, whether an institutional organization or a startup, should integrate the Lean Startup method to foster entrepreneurial innovation on a continuous basis.

Chapter 2: Key Points

- "Entrepreneurs" are defined as visionary employees that exist in companies of all sizes, whether startups or Fortune 500 companies.

- To empower entrepreneurs to drive innovation, leadership should implement Lean Startup techniques.

- Continually cultivating entrepreneurship is the only viable path to long-term economic growth.

3

LEARN

Overview

Traditional institutions measure productivity by evaluating whether or not milestones are executed against predicted projections. When building a product in the uncertain conditions that often exist in early-stage ventures, however, this method of measurement is unlikely to accurately measure progress.

The act of learning is a critical variable in productivity measurement, and should be considered as such. The Lean Startup's method of *validated learning* provides not only a process for learning, but also a way to assess which lessons have contributed value and which have not.

"Validated learning is not after-the-fact rationalization or a good story designed to hide failure. It is a rigorous method for demonstrating progress when one is embedded in the soil of extreme uncertainty in which startups grow."

— Eric Ries, *The Lean Startup*

Chapter Summary

In a world where a wide variety of products can be built with enough time and money, the real question entrepreneurs must ask themselves is, "Should it be built?"

Enraptured by their own vision, entrepreneurs often fail to recognize truths about their new product. They tend to believe strongly in their vision without supporting it with real data from their employees and, more importantly, their customers. This course most often results in wasted effort, time, and money. Instead, entrepreneurs must learn what customers actually want and adjust their strategy accordingly.

To put this practice into action, entrepreneurs should continuously incorporate validated learning into their product development cycles. Validated learning is the process of testing product hypotheses with empirical, customer-based experiments. The knowledge generated by these experiments arms a startup with accurate information on their progress, or lack thereof, toward building a product that customers actually want. By running validated learning experiments, entrepreneurs can identify the efforts that generate value for customers and discard those that do not.

With a validated learning process, progress and productivity can be measured against real-world customer feedback instead of traditional projection-based milestones. In early-stage ventures of any size or scale, an entrepreneur's ability to adhere to this process often separates success from failure.

"Positive changes in [customer] metrics became the quantitative validation that our learning was real. This was critically important because we [IMVU] could show our stakeholders—employees, investors, and ourselves— that we were making progress, not deluding ourselves."

— Eric Ries, *The Lean Startup*

Chapter 3: Key Points

- When initiating product development, entrepreneurs should ask if a product "should" be built, not if it "can" be built.

- To assess whether or not a product should be built, entrepreneurs should run *validated learning* experiments to assess customer demand for the product.

- For early stage ventures with uncertain conditions, progress should be measured in terms of the customer feedback gathered from validated learning, not projected milestones.

EXPERIMENT

Overview

True startup productivity is achieved through validated learning, not merely the execution of a well-researched plan. So, the question remains: "How does an entrepreneur achieve validated learning and understand what a customer actually desires in a product?" The answer lies in experimentation.

Well-designed experiments should test a product on customers, provide insights on how to modify the product to meet customer demand, and inform the process of scaling the resulting product for a large audience.

"The Lean Startup methodology reconceives a startup's efforts as experiments that test its strategy to see which parts are brilliant and which are crazy. A true experiment follows the scientific method."

— Eric Ries, *The Lean Startup*

Chapter Summary

A startup's goal is to build a sustainable business around its vision. The Lean Startup method aims to achieve this goal by refining a startup's vision to align with the actual needs of a customer. This begins by testing a hypothesis on a small batch of customers to achieve realistic feedback ("validated learning," from the previous chapter) that will help guide strategy. This is the process of experimentation.

Successful startup experimentation follows the scientific method: It begins with a clear hypothesis that outlines predicted outcomes, and then tests that hypothesis with empirical customer experiments. The most effective hypotheses will have two components, which Ries identifies as the *value hypothesis* and the *growth hypothesis*.

The value hypothesis answers the question, "Does the product provide value to the customers using it?" The growth hypothesis is more concerned with how customers will discover the product, and subsequently, how the product will spread or grow virally.

To test these hypotheses, a startup must deploy a minimum viable product (the subject of Chapter 6) to a small number of early adopters and employees. Ideal early adopters already possess a need for the product, are likely to forgive initial shortfalls, and tend to enjoy providing feedback. The entrepreneurs should then assess their value and growth hypotheses in light of the feedback from these early adopters.

"By the time that product is ready to be distributed widely, it will already have established customers. It will have solved real problems and offer detailed specification for what needs to be built."

— Eric Ries, *The Lean Startup*

In the likely event that an experiment disqualifies and/or redefines any hypotheses, the entrepreneurs should utilize the experiment's qualitative user feedback to modify the product. If, on the other hand, the hypotheses are validated by the experiment, then the entrepreneurs should repeat the process with a refined, optimized hypothesis. This continued cycle of experimentation will ultimately steer a startup towards the goal of achieving a viable product.

Chapter 4: Key Points

- A startup should design experiments to test its product hypotheses with customer feedback.

- Ideal product hypotheses have two components: a *value hypothesis* that measures how valuable customers find the product, and a *growth hypothesis* that measures the extent to which customers can discover and spread the product.

- Upon completing an experiment, a startup should modify and/or optimize its product hypotheses and then test them with a new experiment.

LEAP

Overview

Traditional business plans rely on a variety of assumptions, such as revenue and user adoption projections, to develop a strategy to achieve the company's vision. Entrepreneurs, however, are operating under uncertain conditions; therefore, it is essential to test these assumptions as early as possible and separate realistic projections from unrealistic ones.

As discussed in previous chapters, the Lean Startup method teaches entrepreneurs to conduct validated learning experiments developed to accurately test assumptions. To do so most effectively, the best means for determining whether there is in fact demand for a product is to "leap" from business plan assumptions to direct customer lessons.

"A startup's earliest strategic plans are likely to be hunch- or intuition-guided, and that is a good thing. To translate those instincts into data, entrepreneurs must, in Steve Blank's famous phrase, 'get out of the building' and start learning."

— Eric Ries, *The Lean Startup*

Chapter Summary

Customer feedback achieved though real-world experimentation is the most efficient method to test a startup's assumptions. This method is known as *genchi gembutsu* within the Toyota Production System, which means, "go and see for yourself."

Entrepreneurs rest their venture's success on their unproven assumptions, which is why Ries determines them to be *leaps of faith*. These leaps of faith initially construct a strategy based solely on intuition; therefore, it is essential for a startup to quickly validate and/or invalidate this intuition with actual, real-world data. This process is achieved through the process of leap-of-faith validation.

In order to accurately achieve leap-of-faith validation, entrepreneurs must undertake two challenges. The first challenge, according to Ries, is to build an organization that can systematically test assumptions. The second challenge is to administer the tests without losing sight of the company's overarching vision.

While administering these tests, startups must also be careful not to fall into what Ries calls *analysis paralysis,* or an inability to act on the data that they capture. The process of capturing customer data, and then creating and/or refining hypotheses accordingly, is only useful if it ultimately informs the production and completion of a product. To avoid the trap of never actually building a product, startups must focus on quickly deploying a minimum viable product, which is described in Chapter 6.

"The goal of such early contact with customers is not to gain definitive answers. Instead, it is to clarify at a basic, coarse level that we understand our potential customer and what problems they have. With that understanding, we can craft a customer archetype, a brief document that seeks to humanize the proposed target customer."

— Eric Ries, *The Lean Startup*

Experimentation, or firsthand customer knowledge, allows a startup to ask leap-of-faith questions. Startups should ask, "Does the customer have a significant problem worth solving?" To answer this question, a startup must engage in experimentation, which yields quantitative and qualitative metrics. These metrics should then be aimed at steering product development towards the needs of the consumer.

Chapter 5: Key Points

- *Experimentation* is the process of converting unproven *leap-of-faith* assumptions into actual data.

- Startups must construct an organization that can systematically test assumptions without losing sight of the company's overarching vision.

- Too much testing and too little production can be a bad thing; startups must avoid the inaction of *analysis paralysis* and put the data from their tests into action.

TEST

Overview

The Lean Startup method teaches entrepreneurs that quick iterations of the Build-Measure-Learn feedback loop will enable and increase validated learning. But the question that has yet to be fully answered is, "At what point does a startup test its product?"

The fastest way to achieve validated learning, according to Ries, is to test a *minimum viable product* (MVP) on the customer. The MVP is a product that has the minimum amount of features required for it to be deployed to customers and produce validated learning. The goal of this concept is to minimize resources spent on building products that have yet to demonstrate customer adoption.

"It [the MVP] is not necessarily the smallest product imaginable, though; it is simply the fastest way to get through the Build-Measure-Learn feedback loop with the minimum amount of effort."

— Eric Ries, *The Lean Startup*

Chapter Summary

Traditional business development launches a product when it has reached near-perfection, but what use is a perfect product if it doesn't meet the market's demands? A startup is innovating under conditions of extreme uncertainty; therefore, the likelihood a product will fail is high. This is why the role of the MVP is essential.

A learning tool first and foremost, an MVP should be tested during the various stages of development, from an advertisement for a product that does not yet exist to an early prototype launched under a fictitious brand name. The goal of an MVP is to test a startup's fundamental business hypothesis and initiate the process of learning from customers. Consequently, the only features it requires are those that are absolutely necessary for achieving validated learning; everything else is a waste.

The idea that a startup's success rests on the launch of a less-than-perfect product may appear to be counterintuitive thinking for an entrepreneur. However, as the author states, "If we do not know who the customer is, we do not know what quality is." Design and quality will eventually evolve over time, but only as a result of validated learning. Insightful customer feedback can adjust a startup's strategy and transform a low-quality MVP into a high-quality product.

"Finally, it helps to prepare for the fact that MVPs often result in bad news. Unlike traditional concept tests or prototypes, they are designed to speak to the full range of business questions, not just the design and technical ones, and they often provide a needed dose of reality."

— Eric Ries, *The Lean Startup*

An MVP that brings bad news is not a failure; rather, it is a learning tool that always succeeds if it has generated actionable customer feedback. It will frequently take multiple iterations of an MVP before a startup can accurately assess if progress was made. This process of assessment is the basis for *innovation accounting,* a concept to be discussed in the next chapter.

Chapter 6: Key Points

- A *minimum viable product* (MVP) is a product that has the minimum amount of features required for it to be deployed and produce validated learning

- The goal of an MVP is to test business hypotheses within the *Build-Measure-Learn* feedback loop as early in the product development cycle as possible.

- Deploying an MVP can reduce resources spent building a product that customers don't want and help identify a product that customers do want.

MEASURE

Overview

When analyzing the data that results from MVP testing, standard accounting practices are rarely an effective way of measuring progress. Instead, Ries suggests an evaluation method that he calls *innovation accounting*.

Innovation accounting consists of three major learning milestones: "establish the baseline," "tuning the engine," and "pivot or persevere." Along the way, the startup must collect metrics that fall under the "three A's": those that are actionable, accessible, and auditable.

> *"Innovation accounting enables startups to prove objectively that they are learning how to grow a sustainable business."*
>
> — Eric Ries, *The Lean Startup*

Chapter Summary

Perseverance within a startup can be a double-edged sword. An entrepreneur must believe in its product, but not to the extent that optimism exists in a bubble away from the realities of the market. The Lean Startup methodology utilizes innovation accounting to provide startups with real data and an accurate assessment of progress.

Innovation accounting works when a startup progressively moves through three learning milestones: "establishing the baseline," or gathering real baseline data in its model with an MVP; "tuning the engine," or testing hypotheses with a set of experiments; and "pivoting or persevering," or making a decision on whether or not the data suggests continued product development (to persevere) or a new direction (to pivot, the subject of Chapter 8).

As a startup progresses through these milestones, it is important that it captures metrics that exhibit the "three A's." The first of the three types, *actionable metrics,* demonstrate a clear cause and effect, as opposed to *vanity metrics,* which express an effect (such as an increase in customer subscriptions) without identifying the cause. *Accessible metrics,* the second of the three types, are those that can be widely understood and accessed by employees, whether senior management or junior team members. Finally, *auditable metrics* are those that can be proven with credible data.

"Only 5 percent of entrepreneurship is the big idea ... the other 95 percent is the gritty work that is measured by innovation accounting."

— Eric Ries, *The Lean Startup*

Innovative accounting implements effective analytic and measurement tools to provide startups with a realistic assessment of progress. Deciding whether to pivot or persevere (to be discussed in Chapter 8) is no easy task, but efficient innovative accounting can advance a startup's vision from subjective optimism to an objective view based in reality.

Chapter 7: Key Points

- *Innovation accounting* uses the data collected in three major learning milestones—"establish the baseline," "tune the engine," and "pivot or persevere"—to measure the progress of a startup.

- Metrics captured with innovation accounting should exhibit the "three A's": *actionable, accessible,* and *auditable.*

- With the data obtained through the innovation accounting method, a startup can objectively decide whether to "pivot or persevere."

8

PIVOT (OR PERSEVERE)

Overview

Innovation accounting provides startups with the potential for a faster, more realistic assessment of its progress towards a successful product. In the first step of the innovation accounting method, a startup builds an MVP to test the "baseline." The startup then "tunes the engine" by testing product hypotheses with validated learning experiments. Finally, a startup arrives at a critical question: "Is it time to pivot, or persevere?"

A *pivot* is when a startup evaluates the results of its validated learning experiments and decides to change its product direction. Pivots can take many forms, ranging from a "Zoom-in Pivot"—which turns a single successful feature into a whole product—to a "Technology Pivot," in which a product achieves the same solution with completely new technology. What all pivots have in common, however, is their goal of establishing a new hypothesis that reroutes unproductive efforts toward a new, more promising product direction.

---

*"My goal in advocating a scientific approach
to the creation of startups is to channel human
creativity into its most productive form, and
there is no bigger destroyer of creative potential
than the misguided decision to persevere."*

— Eric Ries, *The Lean Startup*

Chapter Summary

Many startups waste time and resources because they believe success is just around the corner. With adherence to innovation accounting and repeated testing of an MVP, however, this wasted time can be minimized with a pivot.

When considering a pivot, Ries identifies four considerations to take into account. First: a startup should measure its *runway*, or amount of time left before the company runs out of money, by the number of pivots it can still make. Second: pivots, and the acknowledgement of a failed product direction, require immense courage to undertake. Third: the meeting to discuss the pivot with employees requires joint, active participation from both the product development and business leadership teams. Fourth: failure to pivot is a mistake that even successful companies make; choosing not to pivot because things are going well can result in missing even bigger opportunities.

Pivots come in many variations, ranging from minor to dramatic changes. They include the following types:

- **Zoom-in Pivot**: A single feature in the product becomes the entire product.

- *Zoom-out Pivot:* The entire product becomes a single feature of a larger product.
- *Customer Segment Pivot:* The product is validated to solve a problem for customers, but the customer turns out to be in a different segment than expected.
- *Customer Need Pivot:* The company comes to understand the customer very well, and in the process realizes that they have a different need than originally hypothesized.
- *Platform Pivot:* A product changes from being a platform to an application, or an application to a platform.
- *Business Architecture Pivot:* A startup switches from a high margin/low volume business to a low margin/high volume business, or vice versa.
- *Value Capture Pivot:* The way that a product captures value, such as revenue, is reconsidered and modified.
- *Engine of Growth Pivot:* A startup changes to a different engine of growth—either a viral, sticky, or paid engine of growth (the subject of Chapter 10).
- *Channel Pivot:* A startup switches to a new distribution channel.
- *Technology Pivot:* A startup decides to provide the same solution, but do so with new technology.

---

*"A pivot is not just an exhortation to change.
Remember, it is a special kind of structured change
designed to test a new fundamental hypothesis about
the product, business model, and engine of growth.
It is the heart of the Lean Startup method."*

— Eric Ries, *The Lean Startup*

Pivots are at the core of the Lean Startup method; failing to pivot at the right time can result in wasted opportunities and resources. Whether a company is months old or has years of success behind it, a commitment to routine pivoting is the key to consistent, long-term growth.

Chapter 8: Key Points

- A *pivot* is a startup's strategic decision to change course. This critical decision is informed by the validated learning produced though the process of innovation accounting.

- Pivots can take many forms, from minor product feature adjustments to complete changes to a startup's business model.

- Waiting too long to pivot, or failing to do so repeatedly, can result in wasted company resources and missed opportunities, regardless of the stage of the company's growth.

BATCH

Overview

For startups with limited resources, speed is key. To achieve accelerated production, startups should embrace *small batches*, or the frequent creation of small product bundles as opposed to the infrequent creation of large product bundles.

Small batches enable products to be created faster, thus increasing the speed and number of potential cycles of the Build-Measure-Learn feedback loop. This technique can give startups a distinct advantage over their competitors, as it allows them to quickly reveal and remedy problems without a significant loss of valuable resources.

"The essential lesson is not that everyone should be shipping fifty times per day, but that by reducing batch size, we can get through the Build-Measure-Learn feedback loop more quickly than our competitors can. The ability to learn faster from customers is the essential competitive advantage that startups must possess."

— Eric Ries, *The Lean Startup*

Chapter Summary

Small batches are capable of being quickly tested with the Build-Measure-Learn feedback loop. The advantage of small batches is that a startup can immediately identify and fix defects, thus reducing the incidence of larger, more expensive problems.

Toyota is one organization that has had great success with the use of small batches. An integral component of their success is the famous *andon* cord. Toyota workers are instructed to pull the cord as soon as a quality issue is detected. In response, the entire assembly line stops. This action of pulling the cord immediately identifies a problem and allows Toyota workers to constantly address problematic issues. While it may seem counterintuitive to achieve production gains by stopping the entire line, the efficiencies gained by fixing quality problems early on in the production process far outweigh the momentary cost of halting production. In a similar fashion, small batches can produce immediate feedback opportunities for a startup, allowing it to decrease overall overhead and increase the speed of the Build-Measure-Learn feedback loop.

Toyota further utilizes small batches to execute a lean production technique called *pull*. To avoid the inefficiencies of either running out of inventory or being overstocked, Toyota has created a manufacturing system that produces replacement parts based directly on the demands of customers—when one part is *pulled* by a customer purchase from a dealership's inventory, a replacement part is automatically provided by a local warehouse, and the local warehouse then automatically receives a replacement part from a regional warehouse. This pull technique can be extended to the Lean Startup model, as a startup's product development process should constantly react to pull requests to run small potential experiments.

---

*"Remember that although we write the feedback
loop as Build-Measure-Learn because the activities
happen in that order, our planning really works in
the reverse order: we figure out what we need to
learn and then work backwards to see what products
will work as an experiment to get that learning."*

— Eric Ries, *The Lean Startup*

The notion that large batches are inefficient seems unconventional, but producing a large batch has a higher risk of causing a startup to incur costly delays and rework on a larger scale. Ries calls this the *large-batch death spiral*. In comparison, small batches are advantageous because they improve the speed of a startup's validated learning and allow it to pivot more quickly, thus increasing a startup's likelihood of building a sustainable business.

Chapter 9: Key Points

- *Small batches* are small, minimal groups of features that can be quickly tested with the Build-Measure-Learn feedback loop.

- Small batches allow a startup to identify problems faster, thus minimizing the waste of valuable resources.

- The benefit of identifying problems early in the production process outweighs the cost of stopping production to implement fixes.

GROW

Overview

It is not uncommon for a startup to experience promising success early on—validated learning, positive customer feedback, and/or outside investments—only to see their growth stall. A startup's cycle of growth does not end with the development of a product that has achieved initial success; the key to true success is sustainable growth.

The goal of the Lean Startup method is to help startups achieve a sustainable business model. To do so, startups must not only win and retain initial customers, but also recruit new customers.

> *"Startups have to focus on the big experiments that lead to validated learning. The engines of growth framework helps them stay focused on the metrics that matter."*
>
> — Eric Ries, *The Lean Startup*

Chapter Summary

The Lean Startup method teaches startups that customer retention and product improvements are the foundation of growth. Existing customers serve as the key source of sustainable growth and fuel what the author calls *engines of growth*.

The three engines of growth are:

Sticky engine of growth: Startups that intend on winning and retaining customers over a long period of time are leveraging the sticky engine of growth. If the rate at which new customers are acquired exceeds the *churn rate*, or rate at which customers discontinue using the product, then the product is "sticky" and its user base will grow.

Viral engine of growth: Startups building products that spread through word of mouth are leveraging the viral engine of growth. Facebook, Tupperware, Twitter, and Hotmail are all successful examples of companies with viral growth engines. If the product has a *viral coefficient*—or number of new users recruited by each existing user—which is greater than 1, then it is "viral" and will grow exponentially; if the coefficient is less than 1, then growth will stall.

Paid engine of growth: Startups that acquire new users by paying for advertisements are leveraging the paid engine of growth. If the startup pays less than the customer's *lifetime value*—or gross margin generated over the life of the customer—to acquire said customer, then the user base will grow until the startup is no longer able to profitably acquire new users.

Most startups begin with a leap-of-faith hypothesis about which engine of growth will produce the greatest results; if the hypothesis is unclear, a startup should spend time with customers to gain further insight. While it is possible to run more than one engine of growth at once, specializing in one is usually the most successful route.

> *"Every engine is tied to a given set of customers and their related habits, preferences, advertising channels, and interconnections. At some point, that set of customers will be exhausted. This may take a long time or a short time, depending on one's industry and timing."*
> — Eric Ries, *The Lean Startup*

While creating an engine of growth can be difficult and require constant tuning, the resulting user growth makes the investment worthwhile. Regardless of effort invested, however, all engines eventually run out of gas, thus requiring an adaptive organization (the subject of Chapter 11) that can change rapidly in the face of uncertainty.

Chapter 10: Key Points

- Initial customers, and a startup's ability to retain them, are the key source of product growth.

- Startups typically grow with one of three *engines of growth*: a *sticky engine of growth*, a *viral engine of growth*, or a *paid engine of growth*.

- All engines of growth eventually run out of gas, requiring adaptive organizations that can react quickly.

ADAPT

Overview

From pivots to small batches, the foundation of every Lean Startup technique is adaptability. A successful startup must continuously adjust its processes to solve the problems presented by current conditions. Adaptability begins by identifying the right solution for the right problem; recognizing the right problem—not just *a* problem—is key.

A human problem is at the root of every technical problem, according to Ries. These problems are often the result of bad processes, not bad people. To improve a startup's process, the author advocates the *Five Whys* approach, a methodology that arms an entrepreneurial team with the ability to recognize these human problems. The implementation of the Five Whys system helps build an adaptive organization that can quickly respond to ever-changing conditions.

"Coupled with working in small batches, the Five Whys method provides the foundation a company needs to respond quickly to problems as they appear, without over-investing or over-engineering."

— Eric Ries, *The Lean Startup*

Chapter Summary

Building an adaptive organization is essential to a startup's success. In the eyes of most entrepreneurs, however, traditional adaptive training programs provide little return on investment. To teach entrepreneurs how to build an adaptive startup, the author instead advocates the Five Whys method.

The Five Whys method provides an opportunity for a startup to discover the real problems underpinning technical problems. The method is simple: When a problem arises, an entrepreneurial team must stop and ask the question "Why" five successive times. In addition to helping a startup identify the root problems, this mechanism allows a startup to work at an optimum pace while minimizing mistakes.

The Five Whys method has two rules: first, startup organizations must be tolerant of first-time mistakes; second, they must never allow the same mistakes to happen again.

In conjunction with these rules, the Five Whys method is successful when all team members affiliated with the problem are present during analysis of the root cause. This action empowers members, builds trust within the team, and prevents non-present members from engaging in what Ries calls the "Five Blames." This measure also helps responsible members learn from their mistakes early in the process, before they become increasingly time consuming and costly. Finally, Ries recommends appointing a Five Whys master. The master acts as a moderator for the meetings and assigns responsibility to effect change.

> *"In fact, one of the primary benefits of using techniques that are derived from lean manufacturing is that Lean Startups, when they grow up, are well positioned to develop operational excellence based on lean principles. They already know how to operate with discipline, develop processes that are tailor-made to their situation, and use lean techniques such as the Five Whys and small batches."*
>
> — Eric Ries, *The Lean Startup*

The Five Whys method builds an adaptive organization by implementing a system that helps startups to quickly discover the roots of a problem before it becomes more expensive. Utilizing this disciplined approach forces entrepreneurial teams to work together to identify both the problem and the solution, and thus reduce repeat mistakes.

Chapter 11: Key Points

- A startup must be an adaptive organization that adjusts its processes and performance to current conditions.

- The *Five Whys* system requires that team members must collectively ask the question "Why?" five times whenever a technical problem arises.

- The goal of the Five Whys system is to quickly identify and solve the root causes of problems before they become larger and more expensive to remedy.

INNOVATE

Overview

There is a common, often true belief that large organizations are too rigid to innovate. Even startups that have grown beyond early stages can lose their ability to innovate as their size increases. According to Ries, however, even the largest companies can exhibit *disruptive innovation*. By nurturing disruptive innovation, creating a platform for experimentation, and cultivating a portfolio of entrepreneurial managers, organizations of any size can become a place for ideas to blossom and new products to flourish.

> *"Successful innovation teams must be structured correctly in order to succeed. Venture-backed and bootstrapped startups naturally have some of these structural attributes as a consequence of being small, independent companies. Internal startup teams require support from senior management to create these structures."*
>
> — Eric Ries, *The Lean Startup*

Summary

To drive innovation in established organizations, Ries outlines three major steps to take:

> **Nurture disruptive innovation:** An ability to mimic conditions typically experienced in a startup can nurture innovation within an established organization. First, the company must secure resources for an innovation team (as opposed to setting a variable budget), but make them scarce (as is the case in the early stages of most companies). Second, the innovation team must have independent authority to complete Build-Measure-Learn feedback loops without requiring approval or frequent review. Third, the members and leader(s) of the innovation team must feel that they have a personal stake in the outcome, whether financial or ego-based.

> **Create a platform for experimentation:** A platform for internal experimentation is a critical component of innovation. First, this platform must protect the main organization from becoming politically involved in the findings and experiments of the innovation team. Second, an "innovation sandbox" should be created that allows multiple teams to run short, controlled experiments against a small subset of customers; these experiments must report their findings via a commonly-agreed set of metrics, allowing for comparison and democratization of results.

> **Cultivate the management portfolio:** An ability to create a management team that can continually drive entrepreneurial efforts

is the key to consistent long-term innovation. First, organizations must treat entrepreneurship as a job title, empowering early-stage "entrepreneurs" to independently create products and hand them off to the larger organization for scaling. Second, the ethos of developing products with the Build-Measure-Learn feedback loop must become a status quo of the organization; at first it may not seem easy, but once it is adopted for long-term use, the organization has the opportunity to sustain continuous innovation.

Innovation is a function of process, not company size. Cultivating entrepreneurial processes can drive sustained innovation in companies both large and small.

"Ultimately, the Lean Startup is a framework, not a blueprint of steps to follow. It is designed to be adapted to the conditions of each specific company. Rather than copy what others have done ... build something that is perfectly suited to your company."

— Eric Ries, *The Lean Startup*

Chapter 12: Key Points

- Even the largest, most established companies are capable of creating an environment of innovation.

- An organization seeking innovation must nurture, create a platform for, and cultivate entrepreneurial management.

- Adopting the Lean Startup method as the status quo—not a short-term experiment—is necessary to achieve a sustained culture of innovation.

CPSIA information can be obtained at www.ICGtesting.com
Printed in the USA
LVOW040805191112

307948LV00002B/60/P